Brands We Know

Sony

By Sara Green

Bellwether Media • Minneapolis, MN

Jump into the cockpit and take flight with Pilot books. Your journey will take you on high-energy adventures as you learn about all that is wild, weird, fascinating, and fun!

This edition first published in 2017 by Bellwether Media, Inc.

Library of Congress Cataloging-in-Publication Data

Names: Green, Sara, 1964- author.
Title: Sony / by Sara Green.
Description: Minneapolis, MN : Bellwether Media, Inc., 2017 | Series:
 Pilot: Brands We Know | Includes bibliographical references and index.
Identifiers: LCCN 2016007739 | ISBN 9781626174122 (hardcover : alk.
paper)
Subjects: LCSH: Sonái Kabushiki Kaisha--History--Juvenile literature. |
Electronic industries--Japan--History--Juvenile literature.
Classification: LCC HD9696.A3 J334629 2017 | DDC
338.7/621380952--dc23
LC record available at http://lccn.loc.gov/2016007739

Printed in the United States of America, North Mankato, MN.

SONY

Table of Contents

What Is Sony?

Monsters want to destroy the planet. Sackboy and his friends must use their special talents to fight them and save the day. But the monsters are powerful. Will Sackboy and his friends survive? Several children guide these characters in the exciting game *LittleBigPlanet3*. They play on PlayStation 4. Sony makes this popular **console**. Its games entertain people all over the world.

The Sony Corporation is a Japanese electronics and entertainment company. Its world **headquarters** is in Tokyo, Japan. Popular Sony products include televisions, game consoles, and music players. One of Sony's most successful businesses is selling **insurance** in Japan. The company also makes movies and music. People all over the world recognize Sony's **logo**. The **brand** is among the most popular on the planet!

By the Numbers

worth
$34.1 billion
in 2016

$9.5 billion
total insurance sales
in 2015

around
200 million
Walkman cassette
players sold over
time

more than
52 million
pounds (23.6 million kilograms)
of recycled Sony products
collected in the U.S. in 2014

125,300
employees

more than
150 million
PlayStation 2 consoles
sold over time

$1.1 billion
in profits from
movies and music
in 2015

Sony PlayStation Headquarters

Two Men with Big Dreams

Masaru Ibuka and Akio Morita are Sony's **founders**. The two men did not know each other growing up. But they both shared similar interests. At young ages, they liked fixing things and learning how they worked. The two met while creating technology for World War II.

After the war ended, Masaru and Akio founded Tokyo Tsushin Kogyo in 1946. The company's name changed to Sony in 1958. At first, the company focused on electronics. Masaru was chief engineer and Akio **marketed** products. They aimed to make products that would improve people's lives. They also encouraged employees to be creative and explore new ideas. Their leadership styles helped the company achieve great success.

Akio Morita

Akio Morita

Masaru Ibuka

An Electronics Leader

Sony introduced Japan's first reel-to-reel tape recorder in 1950. It weighed 77 pounds (35 kilograms)! The company made its first **transistor** radio, the TR-55, in 1955. The TR-63 came out two years later. Sony sold millions of these **portable** radios around the world.

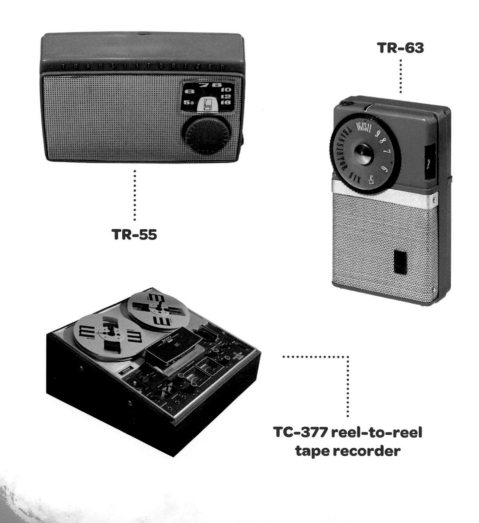

TR-63

TR-55

TC-377 reel-to-reel tape recorder

**Trinitron color
television set**

**TV5-303
micro-TV**

Tapes in Space
Astronauts on the Apollo 7 space
mission used the TC-50 Sony
cassette recorder in 1968.

Sony continued to grow in the 1960s. Television sets
were becoming popular around this time. Some people
watched Sony's micro-TV in their cars. In 1968, Sony
introduced the Trinitron color television set. People
loved its clear pictures. These TVs were best sellers
in the United States for nearly 30 years! Sony also
introduced the world's first **digital** clock radio in 1968.
The 8FC-59 model was nicknamed "Digital 24." Its colors
were black, white, and red.

Sony's **innovations** continued to make history. In 1979, Masaru asked Sony engineers to make a lightweight **cassette** player. He wanted it to be small and easy to carry. Sony introduced the Walkman a few months later. It was the first of its kind. The Walkman delivered excellent sound quality. It was small enough to fit in a person's hand. The tape player changed how people listened to music on the go. It helped Sony become known around the world.

The company came out with the 3.5-inch micro **floppy disk** in 1981. It was the most widely used floppy disk for almost 30 years. Sony then created the world's first compact disc (CD) player in 1982. More than 20,000 of them were sold that year. It launched the first portable CD player two years later. The line of portable players was later called Discman.

It's a Sony
1980s tagline

· ·

Look Up There!
Sony created a giant screen in 1985 called the JumboTron. Today, Sony no longer makes it. But many people still call huge screens in stadiums Jumbotrons.

Sony Products

Product	Year Released
TR-55 transistor radio	1955
Trinitron color television set	1968
Walkman	1979
3.5-inch floppy disk	1981
CDP-101 CD player	1982
D-50 portable CD player	1984
JumboTron	1985
PlayStation	1994
AIBO	1999
PlayStation 2	2000
BDZ-S77 Blu-ray recorder	2003
PlayStation Portable	2005
PlayStation 3	2006
Xperia X1 smartphone	2008
PlayStation 4	2013
Portable Ultra Short Throw Projector	2016

Entertainment Everywhere

Over time, Sony entered other areas of entertainment. Sony Pictures Entertainment makes television shows and movies. Popular movies include *Spider-Man* and *Cloudy with a Chance of Meatballs.* A television show called *Shark Tank* is a viewer favorite. *Wheel of Fortune* is one of the longest-running game shows. Sony also produces top-rated television **comedies**, talk shows, and **dramas**.

AIBO
Sony made an entertainment robot called the AIBO in 1999. The dog models played with balls and barked.

Sony Music Entertainment (SME) owns many record labels. RCA Records and Columbia Records are top labels. Sony produces a wide variety of music. One Direction, Beyoncé, and Pharrell Williams are among the many SME artists with hit songs. Maren Morris and Elle King are also getting airplay. People love listening and dancing to Sony music!

One Direction

A Sony engineer named Ken Kutaragi invented the PlayStation console in the early 1990s. The console came to the United States in 1995. Many stores were sold out of the PlayStation upon release. PlayStation 2 came out five years later. It played both CDs and DVDs. It became the best-selling console of all time! Later versions included PlayStation 3 and PlayStation Portable (PSP). PlayStation 3 offered better **graphics** and wireless Internet connection. With PSP, people could play their favorite games anywhere!

Ken Kutaragi

Greatness Awaits
2010s PS4 tagline

PlayStation VR

Today, PlayStation 4 features new games and an upgraded controller. Its Share Play lets friends in different places play together. Friends can also try out each other's games. Sony is also taking PlayStation 4 to the next level with PlayStation VR. This **virtual reality** system allows people to play the game in a new way. Players wear a special headset. They see and hear things in the game as if it were real life!

Playing for Good

With the app PlayStation HEROES, users get chances to play games against celebrities. It raises money for organizations that help people in need.

PlayStationHEROES

Stephen Curry

Sony Today

Sony products continue to improve. Sony cameras, television sets, and medical equipment are popular around the world. Today's Walkman no longer plays cassettes. It is an **MP3** player with high-quality sound. One version can be worn in water!

Walkman

Alpha a7R II camera body and lens

like.no.other

2000s tagline

Experience Xperia

Xperia is Sony's line of smartphones, smartwatches, and other mobile devices.

The company's latest televisions are extra slim. Their pictures are bright and clear. The televisions can also download shows, movies, and **apps** from Android TV. Sony's 4k cameras and camcorders make photos and videos sharp.

In 2016, the company started a research department called the Future Lab Program. One of its first projects is called "Concept N." It is a pair of headphones worn around the neck. They do not cover the ears. This allows users to hear music and outside noises at the same time.

Serving Others

Sony helps people and the Earth in many ways every year. The company donates money to organizations that support a variety of causes. These include education, the arts, and the environment. The company also helps people in areas hit by disasters. Sony gave more than $250,000 in 2015 to help people affected by an **earthquake** in Nepal.

Sony Pictures Television launched Picture This in 2015. The program encourages people to picture a cleaner world and take action to make it real. Sony also started a program that lets people recycle old electronics at collection sites for free.

Many Sony employees participate in a **volunteer** program called SomeOne Needs You. Some volunteers pick up after storms or plant trees. Others work with youth and help them learn job skills. Every day, Sony works to brighten people's lives around the world.

Sony electronics recycling

Be Moved
2010s tagline

Sony Timeline

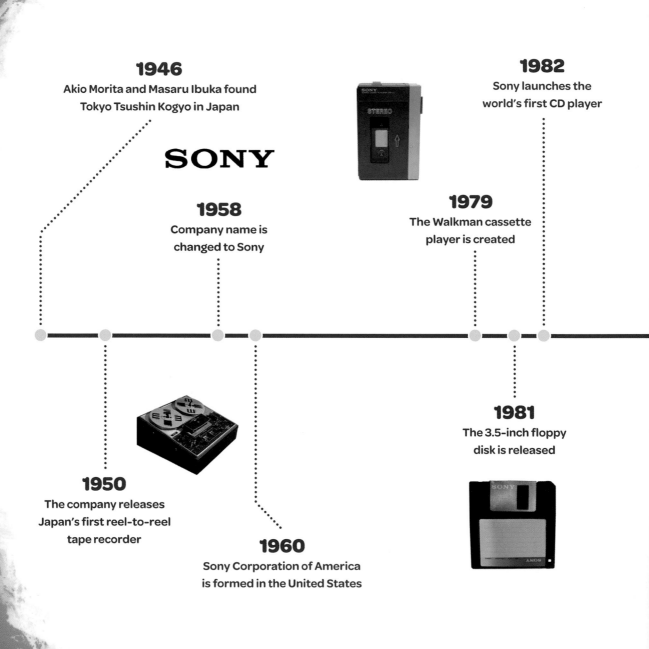

1946
Akio Morita and Masaru Ibuka found Tokyo Tsushin Kogyo in Japan

1982
Sony launches the world's first CD player

1958
Company name is changed to Sony

1979
The Walkman cassette player is created

1950
The company releases Japan's first reel-to-reel tape recorder

1981
The 3.5-inch floppy disk is released

1960
Sony Corporation of America is formed in the United States

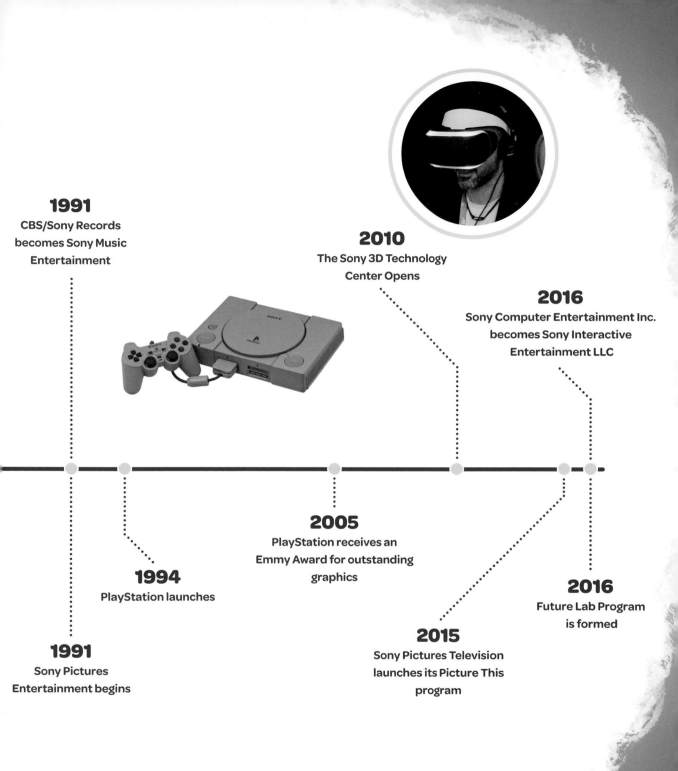

1991
CBS/Sony Records becomes Sony Music Entertainment

2010
The Sony 3D Technology Center Opens

2016
Sony Computer Entertainment Inc. becomes Sony Interactive Entertainment LLC

2005
PlayStation receives an Emmy Award for outstanding graphics

1994
PlayStation launches

2016
Future Lab Program is formed

1991
Sony Pictures Entertainment begins

2015
Sony Pictures Television launches its Picture This program

Glossary

apps—small, specialized programs downloaded onto smartphones and other mobile devices

brand—a category of products all made by the same company

cassette—a plastic holder containing reels of tape that play audio or video

comedies—performances for entertainment that make an audience laugh

console—an electronic device for playing video games on a television screen

digital—displaying time with numbers instead of hour and minute hands

dramas—performances for entertainment that are serious and do not make an audience laugh

earthquake—a disaster in which the ground shakes because of the movement of rock deep underground

floppy disk—a thin, square case with a flexible disk inside that can store computer data

founders—the people who created a company

graphics—art such as illustrations or designs

headquarters—a company's main office

innovations—new methods, products, or ideas

insurance—a promise to pay for losses that could happen in the future in exchange for regular payments

logo—a symbol or design that identifies a brand or product

marketed—promoted and sold a product

MP3—a computer format that makes sound files smaller

portable—easy to carry

transistor—a small device that controls electricity flow in radios

virtual reality—a pretend 3D world containing sights and sounds created by computers

volunteer—to do something for others without expecting money in return

To Learn More

AT THE LIBRARY

Cunningham, Kevin. *Video Games: From Concept to Consumer*.
New York, N.Y.: Children's Press, 2014.

Duffield, Katy S. *Ken Kutaragi: PlayStation Developer*. Detroit,
Mich.: KidHaven Press, 2008.

Green, Sara. *Nintendo*. Minneapolis, Minn.: Bellwether Media, 2016.

ON THE WEB

Learning more about Sony
is as easy as 1, 2, 3.

1. Go to www.factsurfer.com.

2. Enter "Sony" into the search box.

3. Click the "Surf" button and you
   will see a list of related web sites.

With factsurfer.com, finding more information
is just a click away.

Index